D1604572

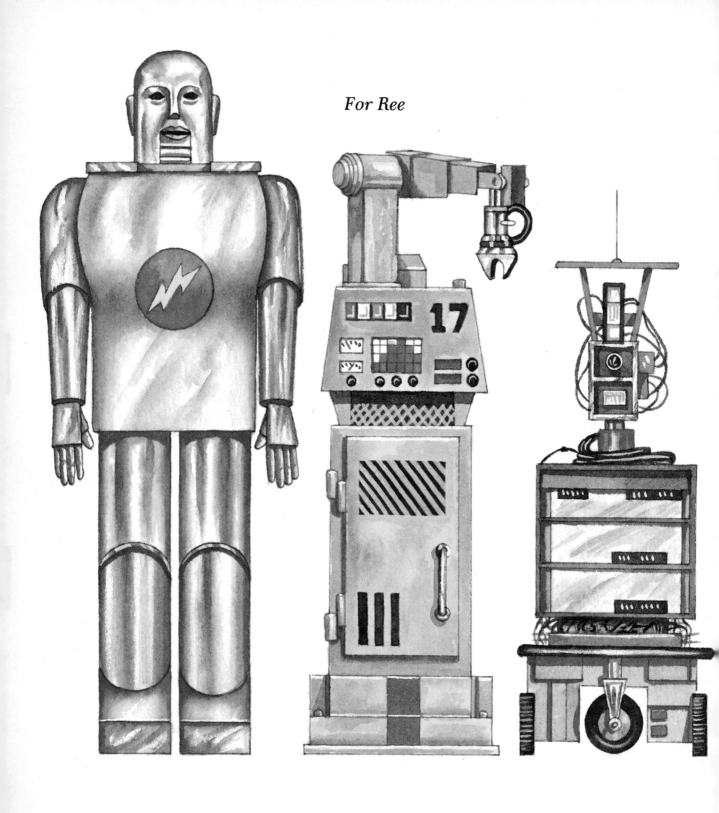

For Ree

Michael Golub

ROBOTS

by Alexander Kerker
illustrated by Tom LaPadula

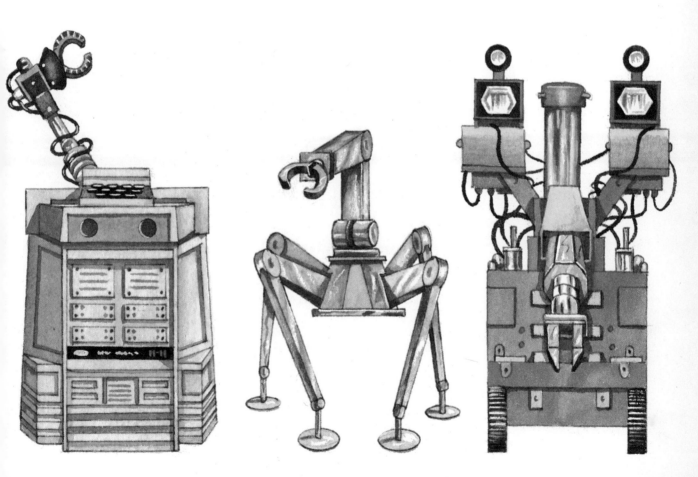

A GOLDEN BOOK • NEW YORK
Western Publishing Company, Inc., Racine, Wisconsin 53404

CONTENTS

WHAT ARE ROBOTS?

Robots are machines. People build robots to do different kinds of work. Robots do many jobs as well as or better than people. They can even do some things that people can't do at all.

People have always dreamed about making machines that can do the same things a person can do. For a long time such an idea seemed impossible. But now people are making more and more wonderful robots, and this dream is coming true.

MAKE-BELIEVE ROBOTS

Many people first see robots in movies and on television. Some of these robots are cute and friendly. Others are evil and mean. Many of them walk and talk and think. They are a lot like people.

Movie and TV robots are not real robots. Inside most movie and TV robots is a person. The person makes the robot seem alive.

Movie robots seem to have great powers. But their powers are not real. People who make movies use special camera tricks. The tricks make movie robots look as if they are doing amazing things.

8

In the movie *The Wizard of Oz,* a girl named Dorothy meets a Tin Woodsman. This metal man is so much like a person that he cries real tears.

It is fun to watch make-believe movie robots. It is fun to think about real robots, too. Most real robots cannot do what movie robots can. But they can do many things of their own. And they don't need tricks to do them.

In the movie *Frankenstein,* a monster is built by a mad scientist named Dr. Frankenstein. It is brought to life by a bolt of lightning.

The most famous movie robots of all time are the stars of *Star Wars.* R2-D2 is a robot that fixes other machines. His friend C3-PO understands millions of languages.

Factory robots can put together everything from tiny watches to trucks and buses.

REAL ROBOTS

Real robots come in many shapes and sizes. But two things are true for all of them. First, robots are made to do some kind of work. They build cars or study the weather or entertain people.

Second, after people start them, robots can work on their own. They are built to choose what to do by themselves. That is what makes robots different from all other machines.

Scientists use robot spaceships to explore outer space.

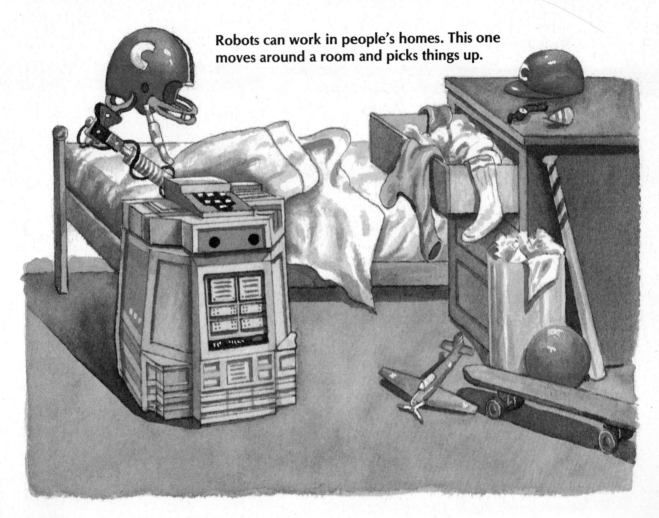

Robots can work in people's homes. This one moves around a room and picks things up.

11

HEARING

SMELL

TASTE

The Five Human Senses

Robots do not have to look like people. But they must be like people in one important way. In order to choose what to do, they must know what is going on around them.

People can see, hear, touch, smell, and taste. All these senses help people learn about the world around them.

SIGHT

TOUCH

COOKIES

Robots must have senses of their own. Some of them can hear sounds. Others see with cameras or eyes. People who build robots give them whatever senses they need to do a certain job. A robot that fights fires must be able to feel heat. A robot that makes sure fish is fresh needs a sense of smell.

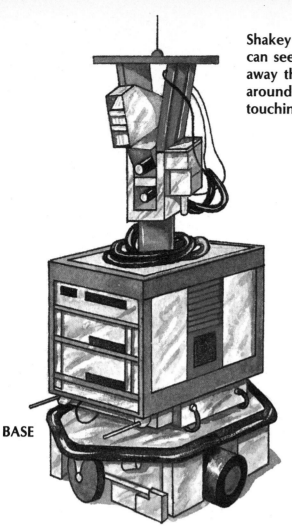

Shakey the robot has a camera eye. It can see shapes and figure out how far away they are. Shakey can feel things around its base. It knows when it is touching something.

Many robot arms can lift heavy objects that not even the strongest person can lift. But to hold an egg, a robot needs to be as gentle and careful as a person can be.

BASE

A robot needs a brain to use its senses. Once it knows what is going on around it, a robot's brain can choose what to do next. For most of today's robots, this brain is a computer.

A computer is a machine, too. People put information in a computer so that it can do different jobs. It might keep track of all the airplanes flying over the United States. Or it could hold the information that makes a video game work. It all depends on the job it was set up to do.

One job a computer is perfect for is telling a robot what to do. A computer can do this when no one is around. So, with the help of its computer, a robot can work on its own.

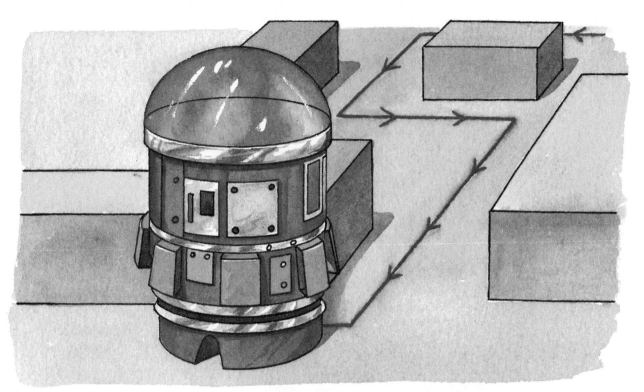

RBX5 has bumpers that tell it when it has crashed into something. It also has a special kind of hearing. By listening to sounds, RBX5 can figure out where things are and move around them.

A computer is not a robot. It is a kind of electric brain.

BEFORE REAL ROBOTS

People first started building robots about 50 years ago. But the idea of robots goes back much, much further.

Thousands of years ago, people dreamed about machines that looked and acted like people or animals. These people did not have the kinds of tools we have today and knew only a little about how to build machines. But they tried to make their dreams real. They built toys that looked like people or animals. And they tried to make the toys move as if they were alive.

Some of the first machines that moved were built in ancient Greece. A man named Archytas built many toys. People said that a wooden bird he made flew just like a real bird.

Another Greek named Hero built other amazing toys. Most of them used running water or steam power to make them move. One of Hero's best-known toys was a merry-go-round. Water inside it was heated. The heat changed the water to steam. As the steam burst out, it turned the toy round and round.

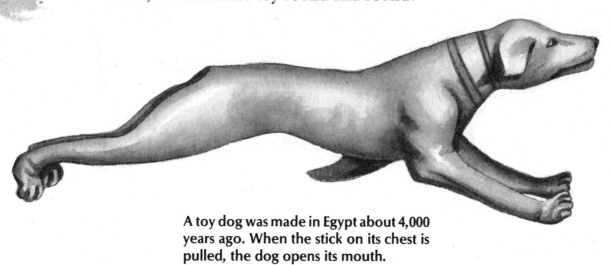

A toy dog was made in Egypt about 4,000 years ago. When the stick on its chest is pulled, the dog opens its mouth.

17

The first metal figure built for a church clock was a rooster. It still works. Every day at noon, it flaps its wings and crows.

Hundreds of years ago people learned to build better machines. They built clocks with parts that moved.

Many clocks were built in church towers in Europe. The people of every town wanted their church clock to be the finest of all. Sometimes they built giant metal statues. When the clock parts moved, these statues did, too.

Giant statues sound the time in Venice, Italy. They have been ringing the bell for nearly 500 years.

THE YOUNG WRITER

A TOY THAT WRITES WORDS
AND DRAWS PICTURES

A TOY THAT PLAYS MUSIC

People were learning how to make different kinds of machines. They began to build very clever toys. These toys copied the way humans moved. The toys had to be set over and over like a clock in order to work.

One toymaker was Pierre Jaquet Droz. More than 200 years ago, he and his son built moving toys. Their most famous toy was called the Young Writer. This toy lifted its hand and dipped its pen in ink. Then it wrote a message up to 40 letters long. Droz could set the Young Writer to write whatever letters of the alphabet he wanted.

THE FIRST REAL ROBOTS

About 60 years ago people made an important discovery. Electricity could make machines move and do things on their own. Now robots could be built.

Two of the first robots were Elektro and Sparko. They were built for the 1939 World's Fair.

Elektro was seven feet tall. Inside Elektro were bunches of wires and electric motors. The wires and motors made Elektro work. Elektro could count on its metal fingers. It could walk. It could smoke cigarettes.

Elektro's robot puppy Sparko did tricks, too. Sparko followed people around. And it could bark like a real dog.

Machines like Sparko and Elektro were the first real robots. They had senses. Sparko could see light. If someone shined a light, it ran to the light and barked.

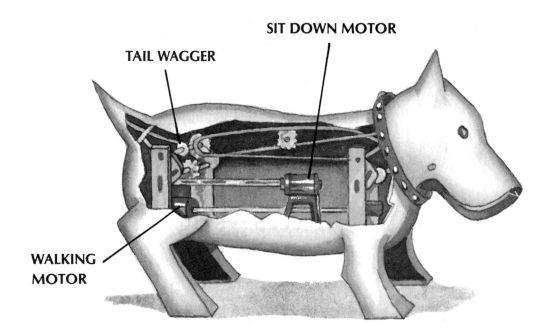

SIT DOWN MOTOR

TAIL WAGGER

WALKING MOTOR

Electric motors made Sparko do different tricks.

Elektro could choose easy things to do. It could walk forward or backward. It could tell the difference between red and green.

Elektro and Sparko were wonderful performers. But they could do only a few simple tricks. Soon people began to build more useful robots.

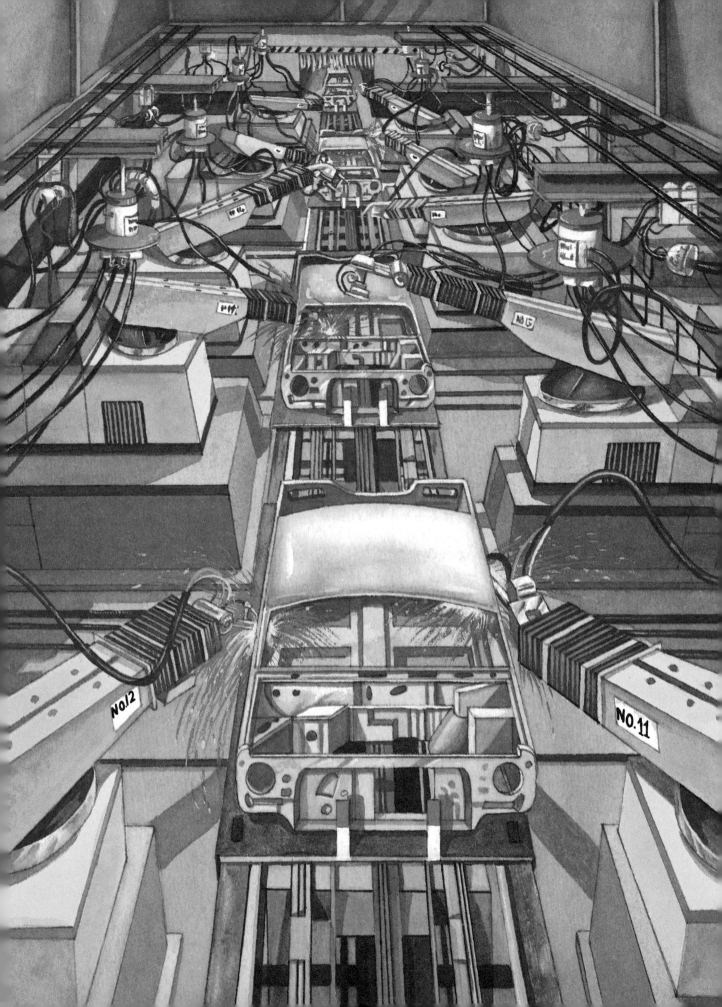

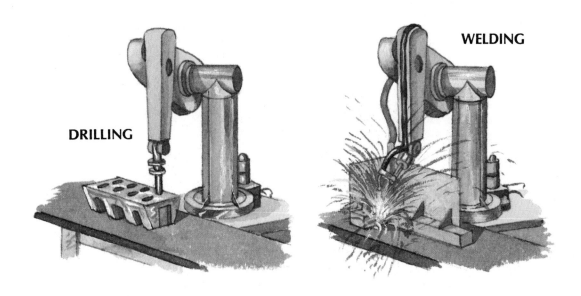

DRILLING

WELDING

Factory robots can do many different jobs. What they do depends on the instructions that are put in their computers.

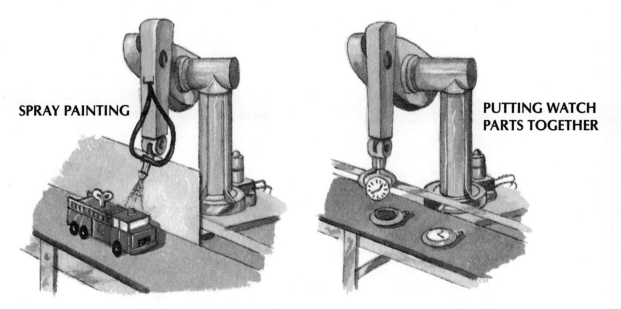

SPRAY PAINTING

PUTTING WATCH PARTS TOGETHER

ROBOTS AT WORK

Robots can be built to do many kinds of useful work. They can work in places that are much too dangerous for humans. They can lift heavy loads and move very fast. Robots never get tired, no matter how long they work. And they never get bored, even if they do the same things over and over.

Mailmobile

Most robots are found in factories. But not Mailmobile. This robot mail carrier works in many kinds of office buildings.

Each morning, Mailmobile is loaded with mail. Then it goes to work. The robot slowly follows a path on the floor. People cannot see this path. But Mailmobile's senses are built to see it.

When it reaches an office, Mailmobile beeps out a hello. Then it waits 20 seconds. People pick up their letters and packages. Then the mail carrier moves on to the next stop.

Century I can even shoot darts that put a person to sleep. By the time the burglar wakes up, the police have arrived.

Robot Guard

A burglar sneaks into a building at night. Suddenly he is face to face with a giant robot.

That is what happens in buildings protected by a robot guard called Century I. The robot guard has senses that tell it when a person is near. Century I can hear and see the smallest movement. Even if a burglar is perfectly still, the robot can feel the heat from the burglar's body.

When Century I senses that a burglar is near, it follows the burglar. When it finds him, it can shine bright light to blind him. Or it can scare him with its earsplitting burglar alarm.

Space Robots

Some of the most important work that robots do is in space. In space there are many jobs that are too dangerous for people. So robots do those jobs.

Satellite Robots

Almost all spaceships that circle the earth are robots. Some of them are put into space to study the earth and send back information about it or its weather. Others send telephone and television signals around the world.

Robot Arm

Astronauts are in charge on the space shuttle. But robots on board do a lot of the work. Astronauts use a robot arm to lift large objects.

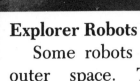

Explorer Robots

Some robots fly deep into outer space. The Voyager spaceships were robots that measured the rings of Saturn. They also discovered new moons of Jupiter.

Mars Robots

Two robots named Viking were the first things from Earth to visit the planet Mars. They studied the Martian land and weather. They even sent pictures of the planet back to Earth.

Children can make a computer tell the turtle what to do. In this way they learn about computers and robots, too.

The Turtle

One of the best-known robots is called the turtle. The turtle is connected to a computer in a person's home. Then it does different tricks.

The turtle can find its way around a room. If it bumps into a wall, it spins around. Then it rolls off in another direction.

Many simple toys can roll around a room. But the turtle is special. It remembers the places where it bumps into things. It uses a pen built into its body to draw a map of the room. This is the way it can show people what it has learned.

A Robot Mouse

Moonlight Special is a little robot mouse. A contest was held where inventors built robot mice to run through a maze. Many mice were built. But Moonlight was the best.

Moonlight sends out a special kind of light as it moves. This light helps the mouse know where the walls are. Instead of bumping into them, Moonlight stops for a second. Then it tries another direction.

Moonlight remembers where the walls are. After two practice trips, the robot mouse can find its way through any maze perfectly.

Robots like Moonlight Special help inventors learn to build better robots. The senses in Moonlight might someday be put into a vacuum-cleaner robot. It would find its way around any house, and clean it, too.

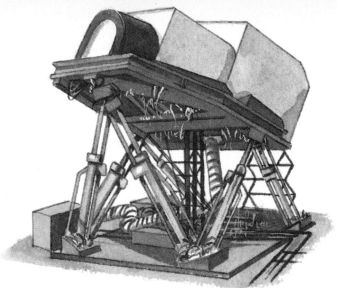

Pilot Trainer

From the outside, the Link Trainer looks strange. But from the inside it looks just like the pilot's seat in a jet plane.

This robot teaches pilots how to fly. It is a little like a giant arcade game. The pilots push the stick in front of them and feel the plane start to move. On a screen they see what a pilot in a real airplane sees out the window.

A robot trainer is the perfect way to learn to fly. It is much cheaper than going up in a jet plane. And it is safer, too.

The robot takes the pilots on a make-believe ride. Each time they touch the flight controls the robot changes things. It changes the picture to show the pilots what would be happening in a real plane. It even makes them feel the bumps and twists of a real plane ride. They learn to fly without ever leaving the ground.

ANDROID ROBOTS

An android is a special kind of robot. Like all robots, it chooses what to do and works on its own. But one more thing must be true for a robot to be an android. It must look like a person.

The first robot builders tried to make robots as much like people as possible. So, many early robots were androids.

Many inventors still build robots that look like people. Arok the android can do chores around the house.

This android tests all kinds of uniforms. It makes sure some keep out the cold while others keep out the heat.

Sometimes a robot must look like a person to do its work. One such robot tests space suits. This robot must wear the suit in order to make sure that it works. Scientists wanted this robot to have arms, legs, and a head. So they built an android.

Harvey is another android. It was built to teach medical students to care for people with heart problems.

Harvey looks like a person. Its heart beats. There is even a pulse beneath its plastic skin. Harvey's computer makes it act sick. Students figure out what is wrong and care for it. As they do, Harvey gets better—or sicker if they do something wrong.

Harvey teaches students about many different kinds of heart illnesses. As they treat Harvey, students learn what to look for when they treat real patients.

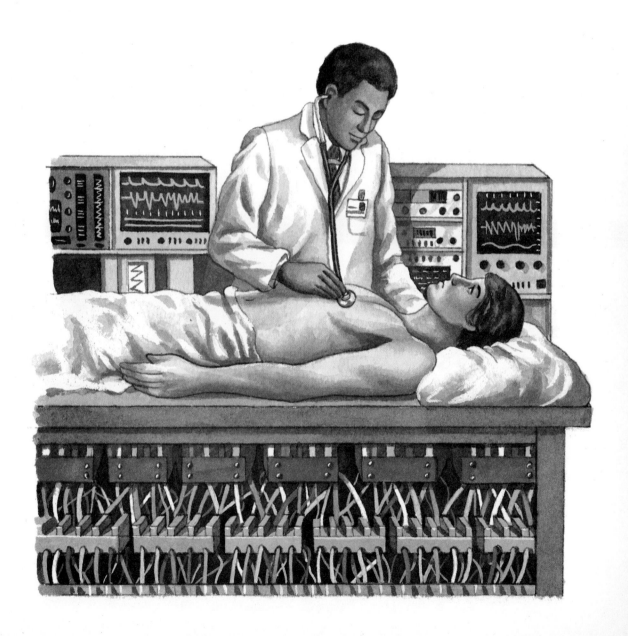

ALMOST ROBOTS

Many machines are like robots. They are also built to help people. But they work a little differently. So they are not robots.

Automatons

An automaton is a machine that looks like a person or animal. Automatons can move. But they cannot choose what to do. So they are not robots. Giant metal statues that were built with church clocks are automatons. Toys like the Young Writer are automatons, too.

A bird that pops out of a cuckoo clock is an automaton.

Many children have toys that move when they are wound up. These toys are automatons.

Sometimes an automaton can look like a special person. An Abraham Lincoln automaton entertains people at Disney world.

Silent Sam looks just like a highway worker. That helps drivers see Sam.

Automatons are not as useful as robots. But people still find ways of putting them to work.

Silent Sam is an automaton. Sam works on roads that are being fixed. Sam waves a red flag all day and all night. Sam's signal tells drivers to slow down.

This drone is called UNUMO. A person sits safely inside while UNUMO explores the ocean.

Drones

A drone is a machine that cannot work alone. A person must tell it what to do. The person sends the drone a radio signal. Then the drone does the work.

Drones cannot choose what to do. But together a person and a drone make a great team.

A drone called Herman goes where people cannot. It cleans up dangerous chemicals.

Cyborgs

A cyborg is part machine and part person. The person doesn't just tell the machine what to do. She helps do the work. The person doesn't use a radio signal to make the machine work. She uses her own body to do some of the work.

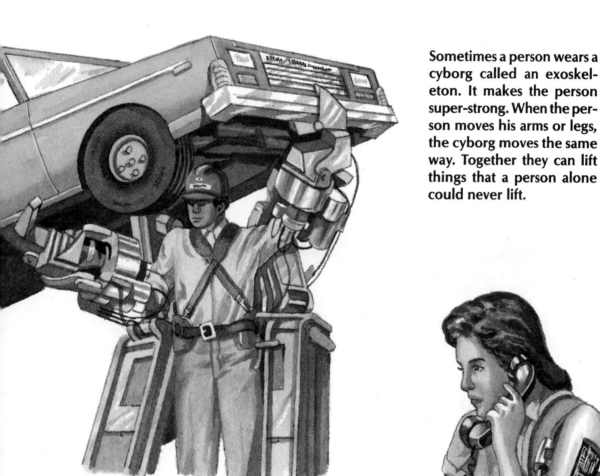

Sometimes a person wears a cyborg called an exoskeleton. It makes the person super-strong. When the person moves his arms or legs, the cyborg moves the same way. Together they can lift things that a person alone could never lift.

A person who lost her arm in an accident might use a cyborg arm. It is attached to her nerves. Signals from her brain make it work like a real arm.

ROBOT ALL-STARS

Heavy Smoker

Alpha was one of the first robots ever built. One of its tricks was to smoke cigars. It smoked thousands of them.

Robot Farmers

Robots work on farms. One robot collects eggs in a hen house. Soon another will clip the wool off sheep.

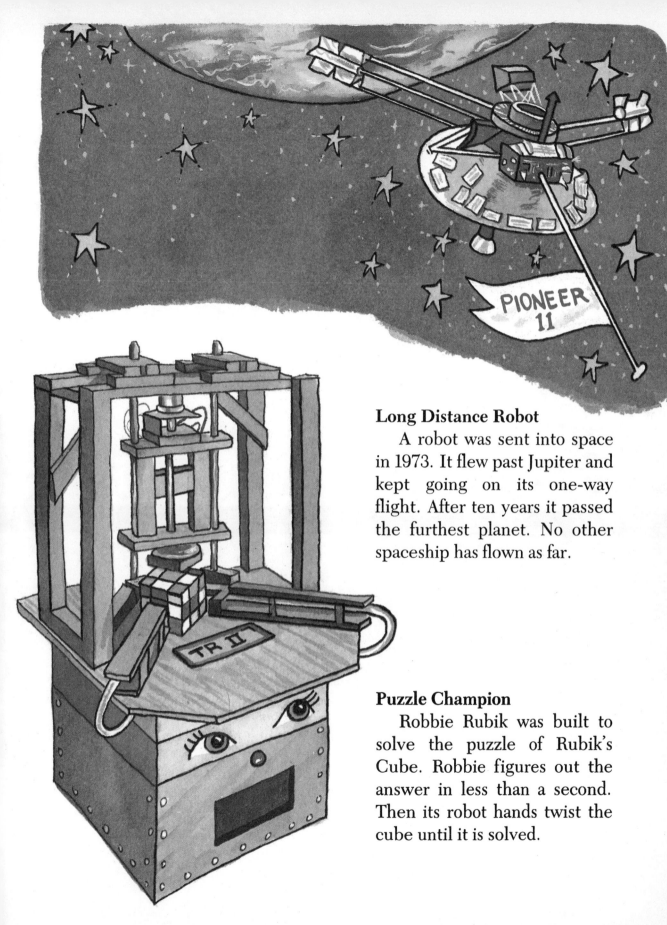

Long Distance Robot

A robot was sent into space in 1973. It flew past Jupiter and kept going on its one-way flight. After ten years it passed the furthest planet. No other spaceship has flown as far.

Puzzle Champion

Robbie Rubik was built to solve the puzzle of Rubik's Cube. Robbie figures out the answer in less than a second. Then its robot hands twist the cube until it is solved.

The Land of Robots

Japan has the largest number of robots anywhere. Over 40,000 robots work there. So far, there are more robots in Japan than in all other countries of the world added up.

A Good Job for Robots

In Japan robots are being made to build just about everything. There are even robots that build other robots.

ROBOTS OF THE FUTURE

Today's robots are some of the best machines ever made. But the robots of the future will be even better. Here are some of the things that they might do someday.

A colony has been built on the moon. There are hundreds of robots living there. They built the colony themselves. Now they are busy collecting minerals to send back to Earth.

It is morning in a house of the future. In the kitchen a robot is making breakfast. Later it will wash the dishes, take out the trash, and walk the dog.

A robot car drives up to the sidewalk. A person hops into the back seat and the car zooms away. As the rider reads the newspaper, the robot drives to work.

All of these things sound like dreams. But robots started out as a dream. Someday new dreams will come true.

OTHER BOOKS ABOUT ROBOTS

Berger, Melvin. *Robots in Fact and Fiction*.
New York: Franklin Watts, 1980.

D'Ignazio, Fred. *Working Robots*.
New York: E.P. Dutton, 1982.

Kleiner, Art. *Robots*.
Milwaukee: Raintree Publishers, Inc. 1981.

Metos, Thomas H. *Robots A$_2$Z*.
New York: Julian Messner, 1980.

Milton, Joyce. *Here Come the Robots*.
New York: Hastings House, 1981.

ABOUT THE AUTHOR AND ARTIST

Alexander Kerker is a writer and editor whose work has appeared in numerous children's magazines. He enjoys writing about science. This is his first book, and he hopes to write others. Mr. Kerker lives in New York City.

Tom LaPadula studied art at college and graduate school. His work has appeared in many magazines. One of the books he illustrated is Golden Books' *Big Work Machines*. Mr. LaPadula teaches illustration at the Parsons School of Design in New York City.

INDEX

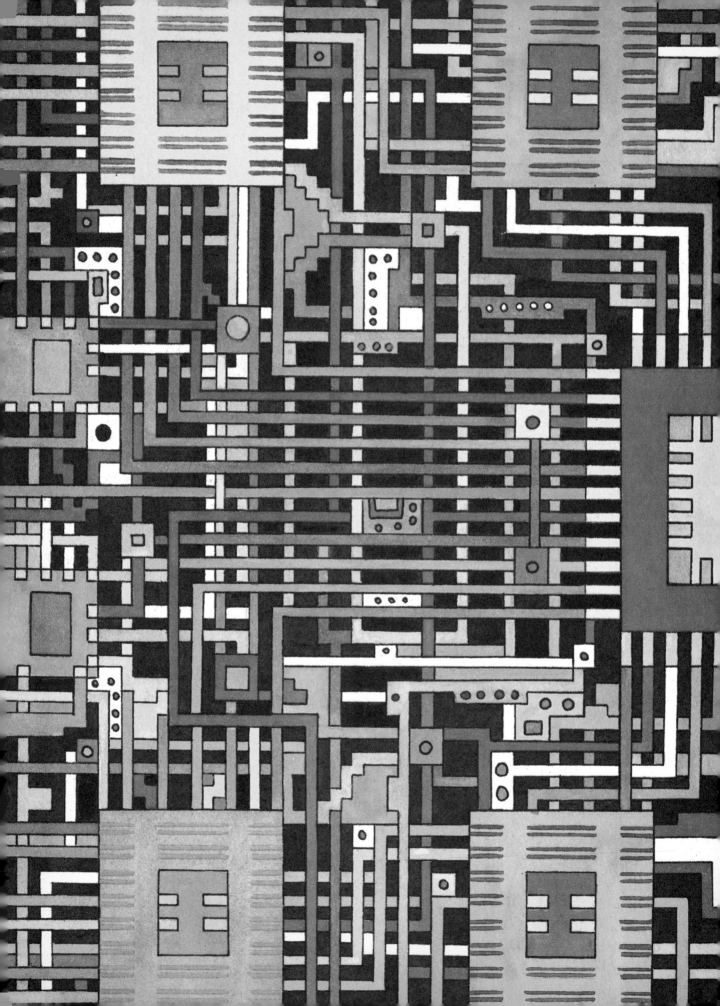